English Code 1

Phonics Book

International Phonetic Alphabet (IPA)

IPA SYMBOLS

Consonants

/b/	**b**ag, **b**ike
/d/	**d**esk, open**ed**
/f/	**f**ace, **f**ree, laug**h**, **ph**oto
/g/	**g**ame, **g**ood
/h/	**h**it, **h**ot
/k/	**k**ey, **k**ite
/l/	**l**amp, **l**ucky
/m/	**m**an, **m**onkey
/n/	**n**eck, **n**ut
/ŋ/	ri**ng**, flyi**ng**
/p/	**p**en, **p**ink
/r/	**r**un, **r**ock
/s/	**s**un, **s**ell, **c**ycle, grape**s**
/ʃ/	**sh**irt, **sh**ut, **sh**ell
/t/	**t**ent, knock**ed**
/θ/	**th**ick, **th**irsty
/ð/	**th**is, **th**ere
/v/	**v**isit, gi**v**e
/w/	**w**all, **w**indow, **wh**at
/ks/	rela**x**, ta**x**i
/j/	**y**ellow, **y**oung
/z/	**z**oo, banana**s**
/tʃ/	**ch**air, **ch**eese, **ch**eap
/dʒ/	**j**eans, **j**uice, **j**ud**g**e, **g**inger

Two-Letter Consonant Blend

/bl/	**bl**anket, **bl**ue
/pl/	**pl**ane, **pl**anet
/kl/	**cl**ean, **cl**imb
/gl/	**gl**ass, **gl**ove
/fl/	**fl**y, **fl**oor
/sl/	**sl**eep, **sl**ow
/br/	**br**eak, **br**anch
/pr/	**pr**ice, **pr**actice
/kr/	**cr**ab
/fr/	**fr**uit
/gr/	**gr**ass
/dr/	**dr**aw
/tr/	**tr**ain
/ŋk/	ba**nk**, thi**nk**
/nd/	sta**nd**, rou**nd**
/nt/	stude**nt**, cou**nt**
/sk/	**sc**arf, **sk**irt, ba**sk**et, **sc**ary
/sm/	**sm**all
/sn/	**sn**ow
/sp/	**sp**orts, **sp**ace
/st/	**st**and, fir**st**, **st**ay
/sw/	**sw**im, **sw**eet
/tw/	**tw**elve, **tw**ins
/kw/	**qu**ick, **qu**estion

Three-Letter Consonant Blend

/spr/	**spr**ing
/str/	**str**eet
/skr/	**scr**een
/skw/	**squ**are

Vowels

🇺🇸 /ɑː/ 🇬🇧 /ɒ/	t**o**p, j**o**g, w**a**sh
/æ/	c**a**t, cl**a**p, s**a**nd
/e/	w**e**t, s**e**nd, h**ea**lthy
/ɪ/	h**i**t, s**i**ng, p**i**n
/ɔː/	c**au**ght, s**aw**, c**ou**gh
🇺🇸 /ɔːr/ 🇬🇧 /ɔː/	h**or**se, m**or**ning
/eɪ/	c**a**ke, n**a**me, s**ay**
/iː/	**ea**t, tr**ee**, st**ea**m
🇺🇸 /oʊ/ 🇬🇧 /əʊ/	h**o**me, c**oa**t, sn**ow**
/uː/	f**oo**d, gl**ue**, fl**ew**, J**u**ne
/ʌ/	d**u**ck, r**u**n, c**u**t, h**o**ney
/ʊ/	c**oo**k, f**oo**t, p**u**t
🇺🇸 /ər/ 🇬🇧 /ə/	rul**er**, teach**er**
/ɜːr/	b**ir**d, h**ur**t, w**or**d, l**ear**n

Diphthongs

/aɪ/	n**i**ce, b**i**ke
/aʊ/	h**ou**se, br**ow**n
/ɔɪ/	b**oi**l, enj**oy**
🇺🇸 /aːr/ 🇬🇧 /aː/	c**ar**d, m**ar**ket
🇺🇸 /aɪr/ 🇬🇧 /aɪə/	f**ire**, h**ire**
🇺🇸 /aʊr/, /aʊər/ 🇬🇧 /aʊər/	h**our**, fl**ower**
🇺🇸 /er/ 🇬🇧 /eə/	ch**air**, b**ear**, th**ere**
🇺🇸 /ɪr/ 🇬🇧 /ɪə/	n**ear**, engin**eer**
/juː/	c**u**te, h**u**ge, f**ew**

Vowel and Consonant Blend

/ʃən/	sta**tion**, dic**tion**ary
/ɪz/	beach**es**, bridg**es**
/ɪd/	visit**ed**

Contents

1 p

1 pen

2 pet

3 pink

4 put

5 panda

6 pencil

2  🎵 Listen. Then sing.

Panda in the park,
Panda in the park,
Having so much fun
Like the panda in the park.

3 Draw the panda in the park.

1 b

4 🎧 05 Listen, point, and repeat.

1

bag

2

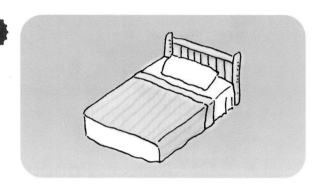

bed

3

big

4

bike

5

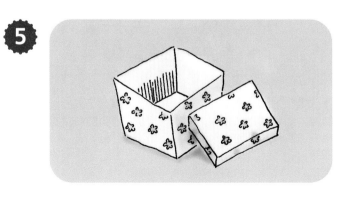

box

6

bus

5 Listen. Then say.

One thing I like
Is my big blue bike.
I keep it in a box
With my little blue socks.

6 What's in your bag? Show and tell.

I like my ...

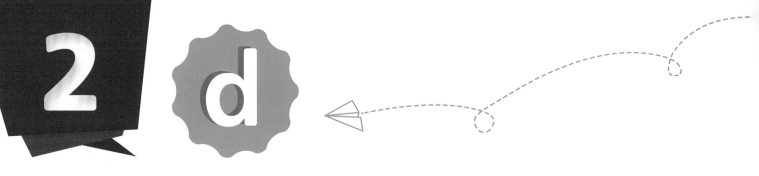

2 d

1 dad

2 desk

3 doll

4 door

5 down

6 duck

2  Listen. Then say.

The doll and the duck
Are in the car.
Dad drives them home.
How happy they are!

3 Act out the duck, the doll, and the dad in the car. Say who you are.

duck ... duck ...

dad ... dad ...

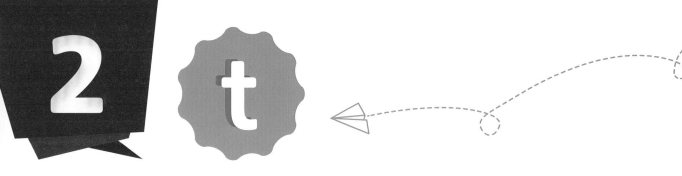

2 t

4 🎧 Listen, point, and repeat.

train

tell

ten

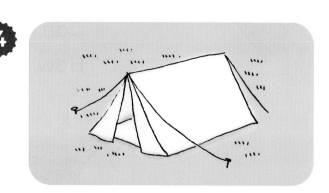

ten**t**

taxi

tiger

5 🎵 Listen. Then sing.

Ten tall boys standing in a tent.
The tent falls down,
The tent falls down.

Ten tall boys sleeping in a tent.
Ten tall boys,
No more noise.

6 ⚙ Act out the song.

Review 1

1 🎧 12 💬 Listen and repeat the words.

1

pen
Ben

2

panda
big

3

pin
bin

4

dad
train

5

pet
tent

6

pink
door

7

put
bike

8

bed
doll

9

duck
box

2 🗨 **Choose and write nine words. Play** *Bingo*.

1 _____	**2** _____	**3** _____
4 _____	**5** _____	**6** _____
7 _____	**8** _____	**9** _____

3 g

1 🎧13 Listen, point, and repeat.

1

game

2

go

3

give

4

get

5

good

6

grandma

2  🎵 **Listen. Then sing.**

Go and get a game,
Get a game to play.
Give it to your sister,
And have a good day.

3 💬 **Who do you want to play with? Sing the song again.**

Give it to Mary …

3 k

4 🎧 16 **Listen, point, and repeat.**

1

Kate

2

kick

3

kiwi

4

key

5

king

6

kite

5 Listen. Then say.

Little Kate
With the little kiwi
Can kick a ball.

Little king
With the little kite
Can fly to the star.

6 Say the chant in pairs.

4 z

🇺🇸 **American**
zipper
🇬🇧 **British**
zip

1 🎧 18 Listen, point, and repeat.

1

zipper

2

zoo

3

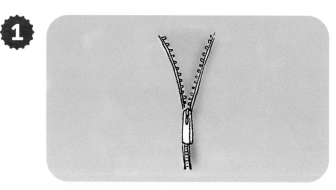

zebra

4

dozen

5

lazy

6

zero

2 🔧 💬 Listen. Then say.

A dozen zebras in the zoo
Start to think what they should do.

A dozen ice creams on a plate,
Eat them now or it's too late.

3 🔧 Act out the rhyme.

4 — S

4 🎧 20 Listen, point, and repeat.

1

sad

2

see

3

sick

4

sit

5

sun

6

seven

5  Listen. Then say.

We all sit down,
We all sit down,
As fast as we can,
We all sit down.

We all stand up,
We all stand up,
As fast as we can,
We all stand up.

6 Act out the rhyme.

Review 2

1 🔧22 💬 Draw the route.
Say the words.

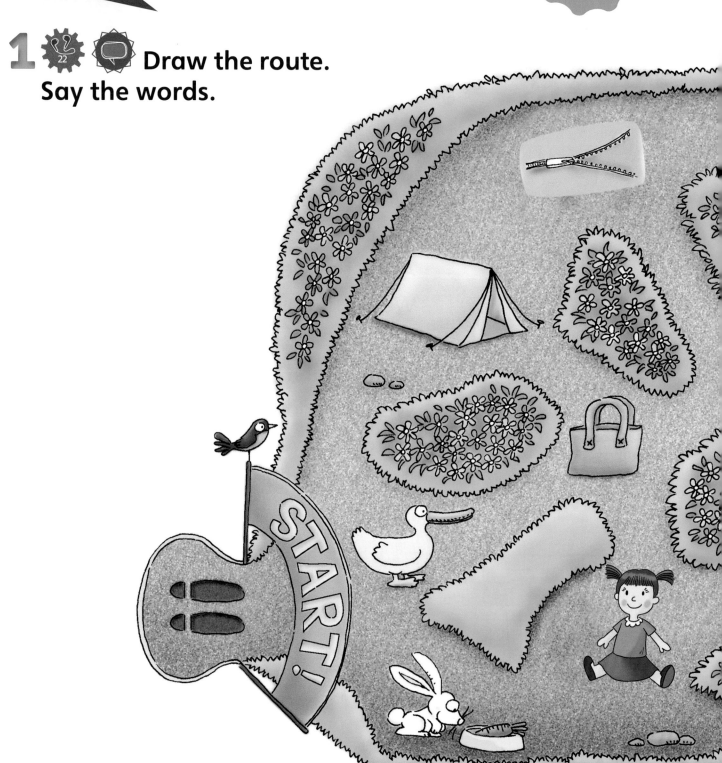

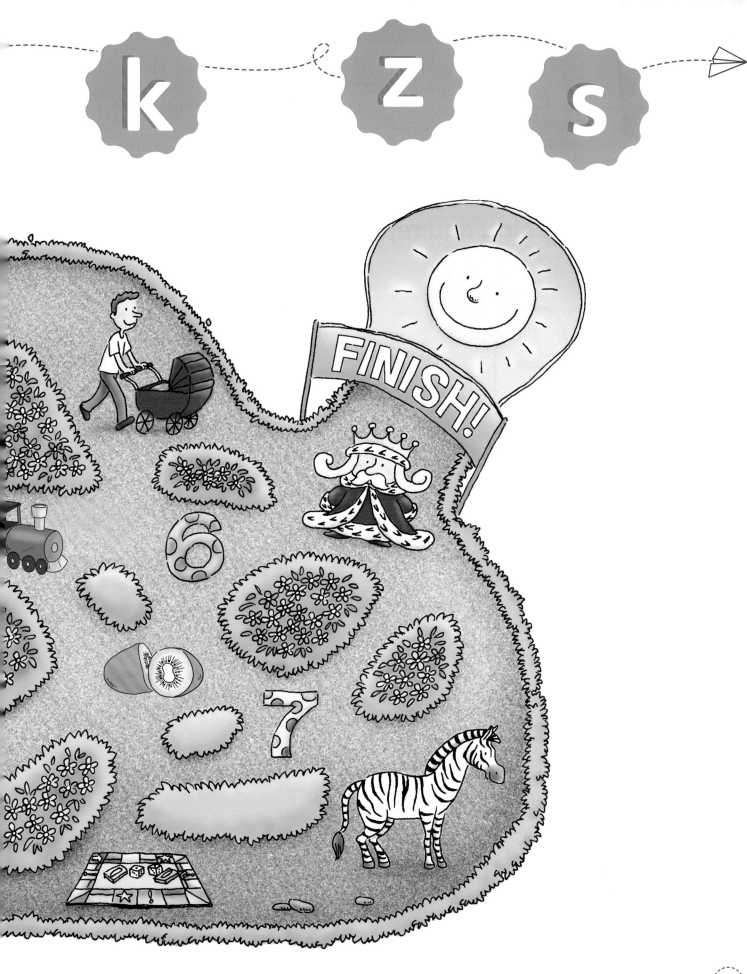

5 **m**

🇺🇸 American
mom

🇬🇧 British
mum

1 ☎ Listen, point, and repeat.

1

m an

2

m e

3

Miss

4

m oon

5

m onkey

6

m om

2  Listen. Then sing.

I can see a monkey,
Standing on the moon.
Clap his hands,
Clap his hands,
There's a monkey on the moon.

3 Who else is on the moon? Sing the song again.

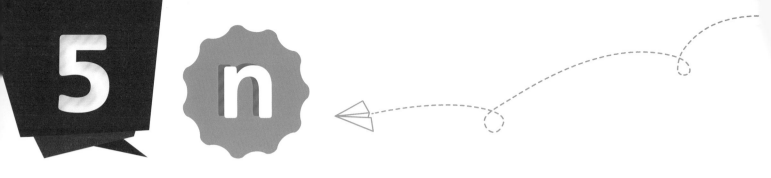

5 n

1 nap

2 neck

3 net

4 noon

5 not

6 nut

5  Listen and read.

 American	 British
take a nap	have a nap

I take a nap.

I dream of noodles!

I catch fish in my net.

I eat nuts all afternoon.

6 Act out the story.

6 l

28

1 Listen, point, and repeat.

1 lamp

2 leg

3 lock

4 love

5 lemon

6 lucky

1st Prize

2 🎵 Listen. Then sing.

Look at me!
I'm as lucky, as lucky as can be.
Look at me!
I'm as lucky, as lucky as can be.
Happy as a clown, busy as a bee,
Look at me, look at me!

3 Act out the clown and the bee.

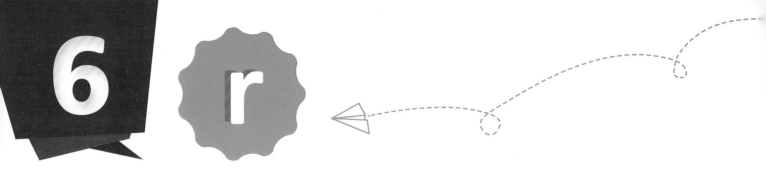

6 r

4 🎧31 **Listen, point, and repeat.**

1
rat

2

red

3
run

4
rabbit

5
ruler

6
rock

5 Listen. Then say.

There's the rat.
He can run fast!
Oh, no! A rock.
Now the rabbit won.

6 Say the chant in pairs.

Review 3

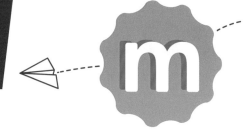

1 🔧 💬 **Play the game in pairs. Say the words.**

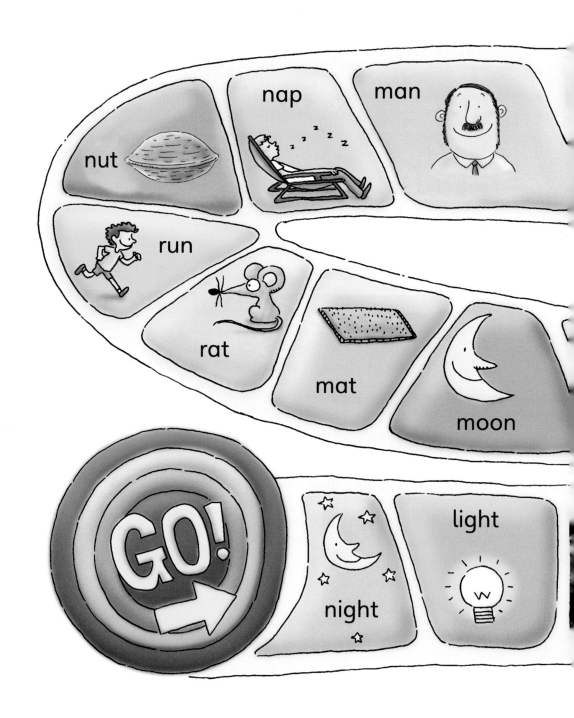

nut

nap

man

run

rat

mat

moon

GO!

night

light

7 h

1

hat

2

he

3

hit

4

hot

5

happy

6

hippo

2 🎵 Listen. Then sing.

Come and see the hippo
Sleeping in the mud.
Sing a happy hippo song.

With a hat on his head,
And mud for his bed.
Sing a happy hippo song.

3 **Say happy hippo as fast as you can.**

w

4 Listen, point, and repeat.

1

wall

2

week

3

wet

4

win

5

window

6

woman

5 Listen. Then say.

It's wet, it's wet,
It's very, very wet,
It's wet and windy today.
It's wet, it's wet,
It's very, very wet,
Too wet to go out and play.

6 Do you like wet and windy weather?
Ask and answer.

8

1 🎧 39 Listen, point, and repeat.

1

van

2

vet

3

visit

4

five

5

give

6

love

🇺🇸 American	🇬🇧 British
take care of	look after

The vet takes care of dogs and cats.

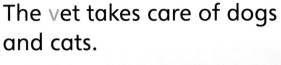

He visits horses, sheep, and cows.

He makes them feel very good.

They all love the vet.

3 **What other animals does the vet visit?**

8

f

4 🎧41 Listen, point, and repeat.

1

fan

2
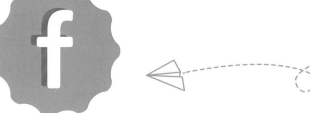
face

3

fish

4

fox

5

ferry

6

funny

5 Listen. Then say.

I can swim like a fish,
A very funny fish,
I can swim like a very funny fish.

I can run like a fox,
A very furry fox,
I can run like a very furry fox.

6 Act out the fish and the fox.

Review 4

1 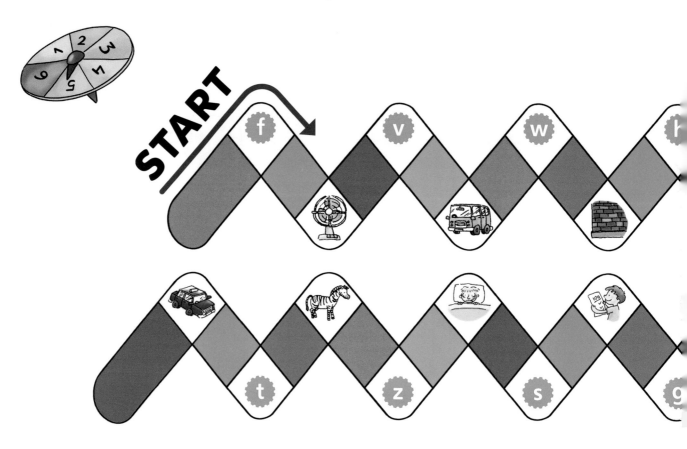 Play the game. Say and write the words.

START

FINISH!

f _____   v _____

m _____   n _____

g _____   s _____

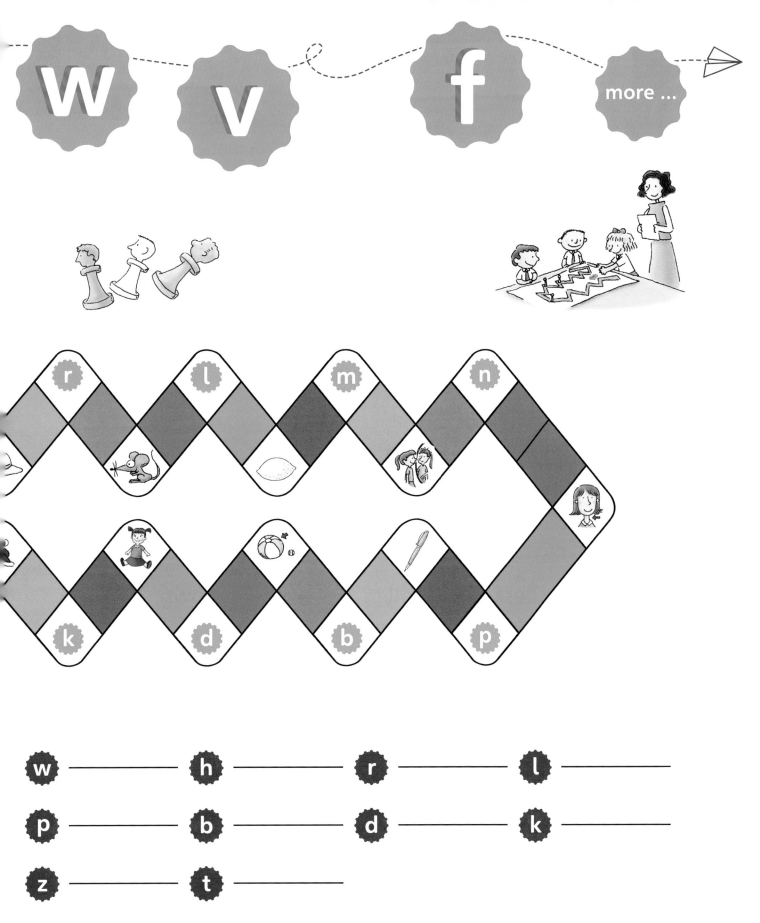

PHONICS DICTIONARY

 p

pen	pet	pink	put	panda	pencil

 **b**

bag	bed	big	bike	box	bus

 d

dad	desk	doll	door	down	duck

 **t**

train	tell	ten	tent	taxi	tiger

g game   go   give   get   good   grandma

k Kate   kick   kiwi   key   king   kite

z zipper   zoo   zebra   dozen   lazy   zero

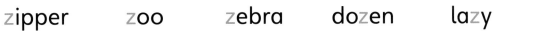

s sad   see   sick   sit   sun   seven

m

man	me	Miss	moon	monkey	mom

n

nap	neck	net	noon	not	nut

l

lamp	leg	lock	love	lemon	lucky

r

rat	red	run	rabbit	ruler	rock

h   hat   he   hit   hot   happy   hippo

w   wall   week   wet   win   window   woman

v   van   vet   visit   five   give   love

f   fan   face   fish   fox   ferry   funny

Pearson Education Limited
KAO TWO
KAO Park
Hockham Way
Harlow, Essex
CM17 9SR
England
and Associated Companies throughout the world.

english.com/englishcode

Authorized Licenced Edition from the English language edition, entitled Phonics Fun, 1st edition published Pearson Education Asia Limited, Hong Kong and Longman Asia ELT © 2003.

This Edition © Pearson Education Limited 2021

First published 2021

Fourth impression 2024

ISBN: 978-1-292-32251-3

Set in Heinemann Roman 17/19pt

Printed in Slovakia by Neografia

Illustrated by Christos Skaltsas (Hyphen S.A.)